Thomas Hurley

THE VIEW OUT MY WINDOW

Daily Reflections from Nature

Thomas Hurley

With Thomas Sager

"Truths are inscribed in the heart by the finger of God,
And remain there firm and indelible."
-- *The Art of Prayer,* by Igumen Chariton

Published 2021.
Intellectual Property of Thomas Hurley.
Please do not copy or forward without the
permission of the author.

PREFACE

For fifty-five of my seventy-five years of life, I have been fighting my PTSD from Viet Nam. I didn't even know what it was, but what I *did* know is that my faith in Jesus Christ was my touchstone. It kept me grounded when my life was spinning out of control.

A few years ago I finally agreed to get counseling through the V.A. I was fortunate enough to be assigned to a compassionate psychologist, who encouraged me to start writing. This task was way outside my comfort zone. I knew how to talk a lot, but writing was different. Reluctantly, I agreed to give it a shot. Armed only with my eighth grade education and my phone's spelling app, I sat down at my kitchen table and looked out my window. For the next few months I sat and wrote something each day.

It was with the collaboration of my café buddy and fellow Christian, Tom Sager, that the devotional concept came to be. His 50 years as a pastor turned my daily observations and thoughts into the book before you now.

It is never too late to seek help, to try something new, to see the world around you, and to share your faith. May the blessings of Almighty God be with you, through His Son, Jesus Christ.

-- Tom Hurley, 2021

DAY ONE

Today's Sky...

It's a gray, rainy day.

Yet when I look out my kitchen window, I see a beauty only nature can create. A symphony of sounds and colors that speak music. Feeling the view with my senses is life itself; being aware of this beautiful view is more than words can express. The beauty of it all is that it was always there. I just needed to gain a new consciousness, make myself aware of it.

Thought for the Day

Beauty is truly "in the eye of the beholder." Whether I recognize the beauty around me is a matter of my own mindset.

A Scripture Verse for the Day

"The heavens declare the glory of God; the skies proclaim the work of his hands... Their voice goes out into all the earth, their words to the ends of the world."
- Psalm 19:1, 4a

A Prayer for the Day

"Almighty God, you have created everything that is. Help me to see the beauty of your creative power today. Amen."

DAY TWO

Today's Sky...

Today is sunny and the sky is gray-blue.

Looking out my kitchen window, the last day of winter boasts a beautiful gray-blue sky. The sun of winter is becoming the sun of spring. I see the changes. Somehow looking out my window, even though I am inside, I sense something wonderful happening, made possible by our wonderful sun. The warm rays of the sun seem to be awakening life.

Thought for the Day

As the warmth of the sun brings life to the earth, so the love of God brings life to our souls.

A Scripture Verse for the Day

"And God said, 'Let there be lights in the expanse of the sky to separate the day from the night' ...God made two great lights – the greater light to govern the day and the lesser light to govern the night."

- Genesis 1:14, 16

A Prayer for the Day

"Creator God, Giver of Life, shine into my heart this day, that I may experience the joy of Life as you intended it. Amen."

DAY THREE

Today's Sky...

The sky today is a brilliant blue-gray.

Looking out the window again, which to me is very relaxing, I am captured by the subtle changes happening in nature around me. Yet everything is in the same place as yesterday. The difference is that I am looking at everything from a different view and position, which is very powerful.

Thought for the Day

Faith is the desire to see reality from God's point of view, rather than from the narrow perspective of my own needs and desires.

A Scripture Verse for the Day

"So from now on we regard no one from a worldly point of view... Therefore, if anyone is in Christ, he is a new creation; the old has gone, the new has come!"

- 2 Corinthians 5:16, 17

A Prayer for the Day

"Dear God, you have made yourself known to us in Jesus Christ. Help me to see the events of my day and the people who cross my path as you see them, in love and grace. Amen."

`"You're closer to God's heart in a garden
than any place on earth."

(Dorothy Frances Gurney)

DAY FOUR

Today's Sky...

The sky is still blue-gray.

Looking out the kitchen window, seeing nature do its work, day by day. What a beautiful thing to see if you allow yourself to see and feel. Nature lets us see that something is happening even though it is very subtle. "Subtle" is very important to plants. Think about that in your daily life... subtle.

Thought for the Day

As God cares for the lilies of the field, so his care for us is constant and consistent. We discover His presence not in the spectacular, but in the subtle and ordinary aspects of life.

A Scripture for the Day

"Consider how the lilies of the field grow. They do not labor or spin. Yet I tell you that not even Solomon in all his splendor was dressed like one of these."
- Matthew 6:28, 29

A Prayer for the Day

"Father God, as you care for all of Your creation, help me to trust in your personal care today. Remind me of your presence in the subtle blessings of life. Amen."

DAY FIVE

Today's Sky...

The sun and the sky create another beautiful day.

Sitting at my kitchen table, looking at the view outside, a view that is so refreshing. Even though I am not outside to feel it, the view excites all my senses. I can't wait to go outside, after I take care of a few household chores. Life has its priorities.

Thought for the Day

As we pause in the Lord's presence, and notice the beauty of His creation, we find refreshment for our souls. In Christ, we find all that we really need.

A Scripture for the Day

"The Lord is my Shepherd, I shall not be in want. He makes me lie down in green pastures, he leads me beside quiet waters, he restores my soul."

- Psalm 23:1, 2

A Prayer for the Day

"God of restoration and hope, help me to slow down enough today to notice the beauty around me. Refresh my strength by the quiet flow of your presence into my soul. Amen."

DAY SIX

Today's Sky...

The sky is still blue-gray.

Looking out my window, the sun is not out. Every tree and plant is in a light shade, resting, as if waiting for the sun to come out. It's a good thing to rest. A time to rest is a time to grow.

Thought for the Day

Sometimes we seem to be addicted to activity – constantly on the go. Unless we slow down and rest, we will miss much of the joy and contentment of life in Christ. Take time to rest.

A Scripture for the Day

"Then, because so many people were coming and going that they did not even have a chance to eat, (Jesus) said to them, 'Come with me by yourselves to a quiet place and get some rest.'"

- Mark 6:31

A Prayer for the Day

"Lord Jesus, even you took time to get away from activity and just rest. Help me today to remember that I don't have to be *doing* something all the time. May moments of rest help me discover my *being* in you. Amen."

DAY SEVEN

Today's Sky...

The sun is out, warming things; the sky is blue gray.

Looking out from my kitchen window is very important to me, not only because of the view itself, but because of the subtle changes I see happening from one day to another. I notice that new life is beginning to be visible, due to the arrival of spring, which brings the seasonal conditions required for new life to happen. This reminds me that God has created the world in such a way that the right conditions produce good results.

Thought for the Day

As God blesses us each spring with the emergence of new life, so by His Spirit, He continually renews His spiritual blessings to us. Remember to thank God today for your *spiritual* blessings.

A Scripture for the Day

"Praise be to the God and Father of our Lord Jesus Christ, who has blessed us in the heavenly realms with every spiritual blessing in Christ."
- Ephesians 1:3

A Prayer for the Day

"Lord God, you have given us so many material blessings. Sometimes we forget that our spiritual blessings are more important and abundant than the material. Remind us today to say thanks for the blessings of your presence in our lives. Amen."

DAY EIGHT

Today's Sky...

The sky has a medium gray look; there is no sun visible today.

With this overcast sky, I notice that everything I look at is receiving the same amount of light. This gives everything an even appearance – very serene, very calm. In the midst of our hectic schedules and busy lifestyles, "calm" is good.

Thought for the Day

We can be calm because God is in control. We don't have to make everything happen the way we want it. We can trust God. After all, God is God, and we are not!

A Scripture for the Day

"Be still (calm), and know that I am God. I will be exalted among the nations. I will be exalted in the earth."
- Psalm 46:10

A Prayer for the Day

"Father God, be exalted in my life so I can let go of the things I feel I need to control. Take charge of my life today, so I can be calm. Amen."

DAY NINE

Today's Sky...

Today's sky is light blue and gray. The sun is warming things up.

What I like about today is the way the sun is causing its light to create different waves of color as it rises higher in the sky. It is beautiful to see it happen. The effect of the sunlight, regarding its natural beauty, is magical. The sun's movement in the sky causes endless beauty.

Thought for the Day

Just as the light of the sun energizes every living thing on the planet, so God's life energizes us by His Spirit. Without God's energy, our souls shrivel and die; with it, they thrive!

A Scripture for the Day

"In the heavens he has pitched a tent for the sun, which is like a bridegroom coming forth from his pavilion, like a champion rejoicing to run his course. It rises at one end of the heavens and makes its circuit to the other; nothing is hidden from its heat."

- Psalm 19:5, 6

A Prayer for the Day

"Creator God, send the energy of your Son Jesus Christ into our lives today. Help me to be open to the guidance and empowerment of your Holy Spirit. Amen."

DAY TEN

Today...

Instead of looking out the window today, I step outside and feel the fresh air and moisture. What a difference! The artificial world we live in can't compare to the natural world. The natural keeps going on, as though guided by a built-in wisdom. The artificial world depends on us for its existence. The natural is amazing and far better!

Thought for the Day

The beauty and complexity of nature suggests that a divine intelligence has engineered its development. Christians call this intelligent being "God." Nature points to Him.

A Scripture for the Day

"For since the creation of the world God's invisible qualities – his eternal power and divine nature – have been clearly seen, being understood from what has been made, so that people are without excuse."
- Romans 1:20

A Prayer for the Day

"Creator God, your power and wisdom is evidenced in the natural world around us. When I am awe-struck by the beauty and wonder of nature, remind me that You are the Source of it all. Amen."

DAY ELEVEN

Today's Sky...

The sky is gray today, with light rain, but wonderful to see.

Looking out my window, everything seems to be perking up outside. It looks exciting. Step by step nature is causing new growth to begin. How wonderful to see! All my senses are being affected. Thank God for the opportunity to experience every day – even rainy days - through our five senses.

Thought for the Day

God is good to all persons. Even the "rain" that comes into our lives is good, because through it we experience different dimensions of life. These experiences produce growth in our character development.

A Scripture for the Day

"We rejoice in our sufferings, because we know that suffering produces perseverance; perseverance, character; and character, hope. And hope does not disappoint us, because God has poured his love into our hearts by the Holy Spirit..."
- Romans 5:3-5

A Prayer for the Day

"Loving God, you are totally good and gracious. Help me to view every experience of life – even the difficult ones – as a gift from your hand. Amen."

DAY TWELVE

Today...

The morning is to me the best time to look out my window. Everything is so fresh looking. A new beginning every morning. What a great thought to remember that nature is a classroom full of surprises! In nature there is a step by step process regarding new growth. The growth seems to follow a natural progression that continually leads to newness. "Step by step" is important.

Thought for the Day

God renews his love in our lives every day, even moment by moment. You may well have a new experience of Him today!

A Scripture for the Day

"Because of the Lord's great love we are not consumed, for his compassions never fail. They are new every morning; great is your faithfulness."

- Lamentations 3:22, 23

A Prayer for the Day

"Eternal God, you are forever faithful to us. Grant me a fresh experience of your Spirit this day. Amen."

"There's not a plant that decks the spring, a blossom, or a rose, a blade of grass, an insect's wing, but heavenly wisdom shows."

(Daniel C. Colesworthy)

DAY THIRTEEN

Today's Sky...

The sky is light blue; the sun is rising a little higher in the sky every day.

I love the view that I see through my kitchen window. At this time in the morning the sunlight seems to be in perfect balance with the shaded areas. Balance creates its own beauty.

Thought for the Day

The secret to contentment is balancing the joys of seemingly opposite experiences. Every experience of life has a beauty of its own.

A Scripture for the Day

"There is a time for everything, and a season for every activity under heaven: a time to be born and a time to die, a time to plant and a time to uproot, ... a time to weep and a time to laugh... He has made everything beautiful in its time."

- Ecclesiastes 3: 1-4, 11

A Prayer for the Day

"Father God, you have created life to be a mixture of joys and challenges. Help me to discover the beauty in every experience. Amen."

DAY FOURTEEN

Today's Sky...

The sky is cloudy; the sun is getting higher....It's noonday – the sun is changing the view. The subtleties of the morning light are giving way to the brilliant colors of the noonday sun. Bold..., bright..., beautiful! The sun, I suppose, is the greatest artist.

Thought for the Day

The creativity of God is so magnificent that even the sun, moon and stars demonstrate different aspects of His splendor. The greatness of God is visible in everything He has created!

A Scripture for the Day

"The sun has one kind of splendor, the moon another and the stars another, and star differs from star in splendor."

- 1 Corinthians 15:41

A Prayer for the Day

"Creator God, from my back yard to the farthest star, everything that you have made is truly awe-inspiring. Give me a sense of awe and worship as I remember who you are today. Amen."

DAY FIFTEEN

Today's Sky...

The sky is gray today, and the weather is cold.

The view outside my window looks brisk. The spring growth is handling the change in temperature well. I hope the cold temperature doesn't last long. Spring weather is unpredictable.

Thought for the Day

Much of life is beyond our control, and therefore, unpredictable. Preparedness, more than preparation, enables us to trust the Lord in the midst of whatever comes.

A Scripture for the Day

"Now listen, you who say, 'Today or tomorrow we will go to this or that city, spend a year there, carry on business and make money.' Why, you do not even know what will happen tomorrow... Instead, you ought to say, 'If it is the Lord's will, we will live and do this or that.'"
- James 3: 14, 15

A Prayer for the Day

"Eternal God, you know the future, so nothing is a surprise to you. Help me to rely upon your presence and wisdom as I face the unexpected this day. Amen."

DAY SIXTEEN

Today's Sky...

There are light clouds in a beautiful blue sky today.

Looking out the window is so mesmerizing to me. Everywhere is filled with so much beauty. It's never dull. Thank God for nature. It is so much more interesting and far more beautiful than any man-made creation. Man-made things seem artificial; they cannot compare to the natural view of nature.

Thought for the Day

Even the most "creative" work of human beings cannot compare to the magnificent beauty of God's creative handiwork. He is worthy of our praise!

A Scripture for the Day

"The Lord is good to all; he has compassion on all he has made. All you have made will praise you, O Lord; your saints will extol you."

- Psalm 145:9, 10

A Prayer for the Day

"Almighty God, you have revealed your creativity and power in the natural world around us. Help me to trust in your goodness and competency this day. Amen."

DAY SEVENTEEN

Today's Sky...

Today's sky is a light shade of blue.

Today I'm in my bedroom looking out the window. I'm seeing the spring growth changing the view of everything. It's just beautiful to see from one day to another how much new growth is happening. In the night, nature doesn't sleep. Nature is 24/7.

Thought for the Day

Just as nature is active 24/7, so God watches over your life 24/7. You are never out of His thoughts or out of His care.

A Scripture for the Day

"(The Lord) will not let your foot slip – he who watches over you will not slumber; indeed, he who watches over Israel (his people) will neither slumber nor sleep."

- Psalm 121:3, 4

A Prayer for the Day

"Loving Lord, whatever events this day brings into my life, help me to remember that, in your love, you are always attentive to my needs. Thank you, Lord, for such a magnificent love. Amen."

DAY EIGHTEEN

Today's Sky...

Today's sky is bright – a beautiful Easter Sunday!

Looking out my bedroom window, nature is awakening. Her eyes are opening from a long winter sleep. As each day passes, her eyes reveal more of her beauty. Winter is giving up her control; the season of sleep is surrendering to the season of awakening!

Thought for the Day

Jesus Christ desires to awaken in you the areas of dullness and apathy. By His presence, He will bring life and light to your soul. Surrender and awakening is good!

A Scripture for the Day

"But everything exposed by the light becomes visible, for it is light that makes everything visible. This is why it is said, 'Awake, O sleeper, rise from the dead, and Christ will give you light.'"

- Ephesians 5:14

A Prayer for the Day

"Risen and living Lord, as you overcame the darkness of death, awaken me from the sleep of lifelessness, that I may live in the energy of your life and light this day and every day. Amen."

DAY NINETEEN

Today's Sky…

The sky today is a beautiful blue accented with light gray.

When I look out my window, I see nature do what it does so well. To me, this is so miraculous: the orderly growth which is necessary for a healthy, mature plant. Such orderly growth is necessary and amazing.

Thought for the Day

God has built the principle of life into the world. He has ordered the world in such a way that this life principle expresses itself despite the challenges that seek to overcome it. God's life will express itself in us as well, if we are open to His presence.

A Scripture for the Day

"This is what the kingdom of God is like. A man scatters seed on the ground. Night and day, whether he sleeps or gets up, the seed sprouts and grows, though he does not know how. All by itself the soil produces grain – first the stalk, then the head, then the full kernel in the head."

- Mark 4:26-28

A Prayer for the Day

"Creator God, Giver and Sustainer of all life, put your Life in me today. Enable me to rise above the challenges I face, and help me grow into the maturity of faith that only you can produce. Amen."

DAY TWENTY

Today's Sky...

The sky is overcast, with a nice spring temperature. We need rain.

Looking out my kitchen window again. Funny, I never tire of looking because what I see is real. Sometimes nature needs help. The yard needs watering and fertilizing. Nature needs help in replenishing the depleted nutrition in the soil. God has designed things so that intervention by man is necessary for good growth.

Thought for the Day

God has created a beautiful world and appointed us to help take care of it. We need to take this responsibility seriously.

A Scripture for the Day

"Then God said, 'Let us make humankind in our image, in our likeness, and let them rule over the fish of the sea and the birds of the air, over the livestock, over *all the earth*..."
- Genesis 1:26

A Prayer for the Day

"Great Creator God, you have honored us by making us caretakers of your earth. Help us this day to live with the awareness that we are partners with you in caring for nature around us. Amen."

DAY TWENTY-ONE

Today's Sky...

The sky has a rainy day look. As I am writing, it is starting to rain.

I am glad it is raining today, because I wrote yesterday that I was going to water the yard. Guess what! It didn't happen. Procrastination got a hold of me. Thankfully, nature saved me. It's raining today!

Procrastination is not good in most things that pertain to real life, whether it be the natural or the spiritual. Water the lawn when you see the need for it. (The plants depend on your intervention.) When you feel spiritually dry, take time to pray and seek God. Don't put it off!

Thought for the Day

The old admonition is true: "Don't put off until tomorrow what you can do today." Procrastination catches up with us. Personal growth requires intentionality.

A Scripture for the Day

"A sluggard does not plow in season; so at harvest time he looks but finds nothing."
- Proverbs 20:4

A Prayer for the Day

"Ever-present God, You seek to continually communicate with us. Help me to be aware of the promptings of your Spirit today, and obedient to those promptings. Amen."

"A house without a garden or orchard
is unfurnished and incomplete."

(Bronson Alcott)

DAY TWENTY-TWO

Today's Sky...

The sky is soft and sunny today. It's one of these spring days that gets better as the day goes by.

Looking out my kitchen window as usual, seeing spring doing its thing. How new growth is happening is so wonderful to see – so orderly. Nature works well. Put a plant you bought at the nursery in the ground, and it will continue to grow. Put a seed in the ground, and new growth will begin of whatever seed you planted. Spring causes the dormant plants and new seed to "spring" to life, doesn't it?

Thought for the Day

As humans, we have the chance to spring to new life every day, growing toward maturity. The source is Jesus. The choice is ours.

A Scripture for the Day

"But grow in the grace and knowledge of our Lord and Savior Jesus Christ. To him be glory both now and forever! Amen."
- 2 Peter 3:18

A Prayer for the Day

"Loving God, through Jesus Christ you are the source of all life. Let the life-giving newness of your Spirit flow through me today. Amen."

DAY TWENTY-THREE

Today's Sky...

The sky is a light gray-blue, with a slight drizzle off and on.

Instead of looking out my kitchen window, which separates me from feeling the full effects of what is going on outside, I step outside my door today and feel the difference right away. The drizzling rain starts to saturate my clothes. The light wind causes my body to feel cool. It's so refreshing. We must not let barriers stop us from feeling the full effects of our life experiences.

Thought for the Day

If we are to experience the fullness of God's presence, we must come to Him in honest confession. That which we hide from God separates us from Him.

A Scripture for the Day

"Your iniquities have made a barrier between you and your God; your sins have hidden his face from you, so that he will not hear."
- Isaiah 59:2

A Prayer for the Day

"Merciful God, you are compassionate and gracious, slow to anger and abounding in love. Help me this day to trust your mercy and be completely honest with you about my sins and failures. Amen."

DAY TWENTY-FOUR

Today's Sky...

The sky is rainy and light gray.

Looking out my bedroom window, I see everything being saturated with rain. Rain, in the right amount, is good. Spring growth requires a steady amount of rain. What a perfect sprinkler nature is! There's nothing that can do it like nature, especially when it comes to watering the earth!!

Thought for the Day

God pours out His goodness upon all persons, whether we deserve it or not. The Bible calls this "grace."

A Scripture for the Day

"(Your Father in heaven) causes the sun to shine on those who are evil and on those who are good, and sends rain on the righteous and the unrighteous."
- Matthew 5:45

A Prayer for the Day

"Gracious God, you are more generous to us than we can even describe. Help me to recognize your goodness expressed in my life today, and give me a heart of gratitude. Amen."

DAY TWENTY-FIVE

Today's Sky...

The sky has a grayish look, like it doesn't know what to do.

Looking out my kitchen window as usual, I see the same view as yesterday, but with a different contrast. This is due to the amount of sunlight penetrating the grayish sky. The sunlight changes the view right before my eyes!

Just as the amount of sunlight affects your view, so in life the actions we take are like the sun penetrating the clouds. Intentional action is necessary for us to change our situation. The kinds of action we take depend on what we're going through. Taking appropriate action can even change our point of view!

Thought for the Day

The choices we make determine the outcomes of our life, even our eternal well-being. Taking appropriate action can change everything!

A Scripture for the Day

"(Joshua said), 'Choose this day whom you will serve, the gods of the culture around you, or Almighty God. But as for me and my household, we will serve the Lord."

- Joshua 24:15 (paraphrase)

A Prayer for the Day

"God of all wisdom, in your Word you have taught us how to live wisely and productively. Help me this day to make wise choices that will further your purpose in my life. Amen."

DAY TWENTY-SIX

Today's Sky...

The sky is beautiful; the temperature, cool.

The angle of the sun is making everything look so fresh and crisp. It looks so inviting. It's up to us to appreciate how wonderful the beauty of nature is. Gaze on something beautiful for a moment, and watch what will happen: a picture, a flower, a bird, or a squirrel in the branches. Nature makes scenes no human can make. It's magnificent.

Thought for the Day

There is magnificent beauty all around us, if we will only take time to notice. The beauty of nature is God's handiwork.

A Scripture for Today

"Praise the Lord, you sun and moon; praise him, all you shining stars. Praise him, you mountains and all hills, fruit trees and all cedars. Let them praise the name of the Lord, for his name alone is exalted!"
- Psalm 148:3, 9, 13

A Prayer for Today

"Almighty God, your creative handiwork defies description! Help me today to notice that which you have created and to trust that, as a part of your creation, you will take care of me as well. Amen."

DAY TWENTY-SEVEN

Today's Sky...

The sky is beautiful on this spring evening, featuring a light gray and blue.

Looking out my window everything looks like it has received a good amount of the sun's energy. The view looks restful, like the sky is waiting for a good night's sleep. Rest and sleep are necessary for growth and development.

Thought for the Day

It's important to know and respect our limitations. All of us (yes, even me) need periods of rest and recuperation.

A Scripture for Today

"Create in me a pure heart, O God, and renew a steadfast spirit within me. Do not cast me from your presence or take your Spirit from me. Restore to me the joy of your salvation, and grant me a willing spirit, to sustain me."
- Psalm 51:10-12

A Prayer for Today

"Spirit of Christ, your presence brings renewal and refreshment to our bodies and our souls. Help me today to take time to rest in you, in order that my systems may be rejuvenated. Amen."

DAY TWENTY-EIGHT

Today's Sky...

Today's sky is beautiful and alive, with white clouds set against a blue background.

Watching out my kitchen window, I see the sun hiding behind the clouds, which are moving majestically across the blue sky. Since the clouds are not a solid mass, one moment it looks shady, and then boom! a bright light starts to appear. It's the sun coming out from behind a cloud. What an explosion of light! What can I say except, Wow!?

Thought for the Day

Like the clouds, which move to reveal the sun, our problems will also move in time, revealing the answer. As the light of the world, Jesus reveals answers to our needs.

A Scripture for Today

"When Jesus spoke again to the people, he said, 'I am the light of the world. Whoever follows me will never walk in darkness, but will have the light of life.'"
- John 8:12

A Prayer for Today

"Lord Jesus, you are the light that provides us wisdom and hope. May I see your presence and understand your guidance even in the problems I will face today. Amen."

"A garden is a partnership between two hands and God."

(William Arthur Ward)

DAY TWENTY-NINE

Today's Sky…

Today's sky features light clouds against a beautiful blue sky. Refreshingly cool spring weather.

Instead of just looking out my window, this morning I had to take my wife to a doctor's appointment. This allowed us to feel together the freshness of this day, which totally invigorated us. It was like our bodies had been infused with new life. The feeling of invigoration is wonderful!

Thought for the Day

Every morning brings us new experiences with new opportunities to be re-invigorated by the love of God. God's goodness gives us new life.

A Scripture for the Day

"Praise the Lord, and forget not all his benefits: who forgives all your sins, and heals all your diseases, who redeems your life from the pit and crowns you with love and compassion, who satisfies your desires with good things, so that your youth is renewed like the eagle's."
- Psalm 103:2-5

A Prayer for the Day

"Loving God, your mercies are indeed new every morning. Make me mindful of the ways you will pour your love into my life this day, and help me to be grateful. Amen."

DAY THIRTY

Today's Sky...

It's evening. The sky is a calm-looking color on this beautiful spring night.

Looking out my kitchen window, everything looks so peaceful and tranquil. As I am looking out, I can see the day changing into night minute by minute. These changes keep our days interesting. It's so beautiful to see.

Thought for the Day

Change does not have to be a fearful experience. How we handle change in many respects determines the outcomes of our lives.

A Scripture for the Day

"God is our refuge and strength, an ever-present help in trouble. Therefore we will not fear, though the earth should change..."

- Psalm 46:1, 2

A Prayer for the Day

"Everlasting God, your Word says that you never change. Help me today to embrace change rather than fear it, knowing that your consistent presence will grace my life. Amen."

DAY THIRTY-ONE

Today's Sky...

The sky is a beautiful blue with very light clouds. Today's temperature is nice.

Looking out my window, I see the beautiful shadows the trees with the sun create. The slow movement of the sun allows the trees to cast a different shadow as the day progresses. The position of the trees and the plants is the same, but because of the sun's movement the view changes constantly. I don't get bored with the view; the sun will not allow it.

Thought for the Day

My perspective on life determines the choices I make. Gaining different perspectives as I go through life is helpful as I consider the actions I will take.

A Scripture for the Day

"In the heavens he has pitched a tent for the sun, which is like a bridegroom coming forth from his pavilion, like a champion rejoicing to run his course. It rises at one end of the heavens and makes its circuit to the other; nothing is hidden from its heat."
- Psalm 19:4b, 5

A Prayer for the Day

"Eternal God, you hold a perspective on life that is far different from our human perspectives. Help me to discern how you see the events of my day, and enable me to respond in accordance with your will. Amen."

DAY THIRTY-TWO

Today's Sky...

Today is a great looking day. I'm going out to take care of the yard.

When I go outside, I notice that I have the ability to work with nature to create a beautiful scene. Springtime is the opportune time. Due to growth from previous years, plants that have become too large need to be split into smaller pieces. Guess what? I am the one to do it. Through trial and error I, Tom, have become a splitter and transplant-er, but it took time to learn how to do this without killing the plants. (This happened a lot in the beginning.) "Sorry, plants," I'd say. At first they were sad, but now they all have a happy face. I think they sense that I know what I'm doing now. They are saying to each other, "We're going to live even though we are being split and transplanted." When the plants see me come out to work the yard, it's as if they see a gardener.

Thought for the Day
Just as a gardener prunes his plants to make them more productive, so God "prunes" the things in our lives which keep us from being productive persons.

A Scripture for the Day
"I am the vine, and my Father is the gardener. He lifts up every branch in me that bears no fruit, while every branch that does bear fruit he prunes so that it will be even more fruitful."
- John 15:1-2

A Prayer for the Day
"Like an experienced gardener, Father, you care about who we are becoming. Help me today to be open to the change you want to create in my life so I can be the person you desire. Amen."

DAY THIRTY-THREE

Today's Sky...

The sky has a light gray look with light snow falling. Yes, the temperature is cold enough for snow!

When I look out my bedroom window this morning, all I can see is a blanket of heavy snow on everything. This gives the view a pristine white look. The heavy snow caused the branches of the trees to bend. Believe me, they are very low, some touching the ground. I had a dental appointment today. In the time I was gone, the temperature rose from about 30 degrees to 45 degrees. This caused the snow to melt rapidly. Thank God, because I think the cold temperature and snow, if they were to linger, would have caused a lot of damage to the young spring growth.

Thought for the Day

Things can change suddenly from a spring day to a wintry day. Even though nature and life itself are unpredictable, God's character is consistent and trustworthy.

A Scripture for the Day

"Jesus Christ is the same yesterday and today and forever... Through Jesus, therefore, let us continually offer to God a sacrifice of praise..."
- Hebrews 13:8, 15

A Prayer for the Day

"Eternal God, even though life is in many ways unpredictable, thank you that your love takes care of us no matter what comes our way. Help me today to trust in your love. Amen."

DAY THIRTY-FOUR

Today's Sky...

Today's sky is a light gray. The spring plants are still recovering from yesterday's snow fall.

Looking out my window, the scene I view looks like a cold day. The gray clouds are hiding the sun's warmth. So far the spring growth looks like it is handling the change in temperature. It also looks as if it wants to rain. If it does, it will be a cold rain or snow, due to the temperature drop. (I hope it rains!) The spring growth sometimes has to endure the cold weather of early spring. It's the same with us: we must learn to endure the challenges we face on our life's journey.

Thought for the Day

Challenges strengthen us and shape our character. Rather than curse our problems, we can learn from them.

A Scripture for the Day

"Consider it pure joy, my brothers and sisters, whenever you face trials of many kinds, because you know that the testing of your faith develops perseverance. Perseverance must finish its work so that you may be mature and complete, not lacking anything."

- James 1:2-4

A Prayer for the Day

"Father God, you know me well enough to know that I prefer ease over difficulty. Help me today to allow the challenges of my life to teach and shape me, so that I might become more mature in you. Amen."

DAY THIRTY-FIVE

Today's Sky...

The sky looks like a day of recovering from the cold spell that is still passing through.

Again looking through my kitchen window, I see all the plants and trees recovering pretty well from the cold spell. Such weather changes can happen suddenly during springtime. I am glad that I fertilized early to replenish the nutrition that became depleted during the winter season. Sometimes nature needs help to be able to survive. Through the years, I have learned so much about helping nature survive the bad moments.

Thought for the Day

As nature needs fertilizer to nourish her, we as human beings need the nourishment of God's Spirit to replenish our souls.

A Scripture for the Day

"I am the vine; you are the branches. If anyone remains in me and I in him, he will bear much fruit; but apart from me you can do nothing."

- John 15:5

A Prayer for the Day

"Creator God, you are the source of all spiritual sustenance. Feed my soul today with the nourishment of your Holy Spirit, that I might be strengthened and equipped to serve you. Amen."

DAY THIRTY-SIX

Today's Sky...

During this evening time, everything looks its real color. The sun and the shade are at equal proportion.

I just came in from working in the yard. Time seems to go so fast when I am outside. It's so enjoyable, especially knowing that all the plants, ornamental grasses, and shrub trees have been planted by me through the years. To see everything so mature is wonderful! I just follow the step-by-step instructions for fertilization, watering, weed control, etc. Life is a step by step process, just like gardening.

Thought for the Day

Through the Bible, God has provided a step-by-step guidebook for life. If we follow its teachings, we will grow into maturity as persons.

A Scripture for the Day

"All scripture is inspired by God and is useful to teach us what is true and to make us realize what is wrong in our lives. It straightens us out and teaches us to do what is right. It is God's way of preparing us in every way, fully equipped for every good thing God wants us to do."

- 2 Timothy 3:16-17 (NLT)

A Prayer for the Day

"Infinite God, thank you for revealing your wisdom through the pages of the Bible. Help me today to apply the wisdom of this book to my decisions and actions. Amen."

DAY THIRTY-SEVEN

Today's Sky...

Today's sky features light clouds. The sky has a gray look because of the angle of the sun.

I went outside this morning and walked around. I noticed that all the plants are still reviving from the long winter, even though the first month of spring has passed. They seem to have a growth principle built into their being. It is just amazing how resilient growth is.

Thought for the Day

Like the plants around us, God has built resiliency into our being. We can deal with anything life throws at us as we rely on Him

A Scripture for the Day

"I know what it is to be in need, and I know what it is to have plenty.... I can handle anything through Christ who gives me strength."
- Philippians 4:12-13

A Prayer for the Day

"Caring God, when life becomes difficult, help me to remember that my strength and hope are in you. Help me to rely upon you fully in the midst of struggle. Amen."

"Trees are poems that the earth writes upon the sky."

(Kahlil Gibran)

DAY THIRTY-EIGHT

Today's Sky...

It's cool today, but this spring day looks inviting.

Looking out my kitchen window, the view looks so refreshing. Connecting with nature is so necessary for my mental health. The artificial scenes we create in our homes cannot compare to the beauty of the natural world, at least for me. I connect with the natural world, because it is real, like me.

Thought for the Day

The "pure in heart" are those who are completely honest and real. Meaningful relationships are rooted in authenticity.

A Scripture for the Day

(Jesus said,) "Blessed are the poor in spirit, for theirs is the kingdom of heaven... Blessed are the pure in heart, for they will see God."
- Matthew 5:3, 8

A Prayer for the Day

"All-knowing God, you are aware of our desire to make a good impression on others. Help me today to be real in all my interactions, so that I may genuinely communicate your love to others. Amen."

DAY THIRTY-NINE

Today's Sky...

It's a typical spring day, and warming up. We need rain.

I'll be outside most of the day. This is a day I will help nature look neat, pretty, orderly, which is necessary for a nice-looking yard. It's actually a very enjoyable experience, even though it requires removing weeds, cutting the grass, watering, fertilizing, and removing twigs which fall from the trees. Nature needs a little TLC sometimes to look good!

Thought for the Day

As a person, I need help to bloom. I need love, appreciation, consideration, understanding, purpose, sensitivity – the list goes on and on. Life is a complicated experience in some respects, yet simple when it comes to the basics.

A Scripture for the Day

"A new command I give you: Love one another. As I have loved you, so you must love one another. By this everyone will know that you are my disciples, if you love one another."
- John 13:34-35

A Prayer for the Day

"Merciful God, forgive me for the times that I get wrapped up in my own needs and desires. Help me today to be sensitive to the needs of those around me, who are just as fragile as I am. Amen."

DAY FORTY

Today's Sky...

This morning's sky looks as if it could go either way: rain or sunshine.

I start my day, as usual, by looking out my kitchen window. As I relax, I'm drinking a good cup of coffee and eating toasted bread with a spread of peanut butter. I am learning to appreciate the beautiful view that nature has allowed me to develop. However, it required lots of work, which I actually enjoy. The cup of coffee lights me up. The toast and peanut butter spread awakens my taste buds. I am ready to go!

Thought for the Day

A good start makes for a more productive day. We often cheat ourselves of that experience. Don't forget to take time each morning to focus on what matters most. Prayer is a good way to gain focus.

A Scripture for the Day

"Very early in the morning, while it was still dark, Jesus got up, left the house, and went off to a solitary place, where he prayed."

- Mark 1:35

A Prayer for the Day

"Lord Jesus, even you needed to gain strength and focus through prayer. Help me today to remember that my life is centered in You, so that I can be about the work You want me to do. Amen."

DAY FORTY-ONE

Today's Sky...

The sky and the ground look even in the morning light. The hue of the sun is soft to the eyes.

I went out earlier with my wife to do some grocery shopping. The open road allowed me to see farther than I had been able to see when looking out my kitchen window. It struck me that the clouds and the horizon seemed to become as one. This change of appearance was possible only because I found another "point of view." Sometimes a different perspective helps us see more clearly. Thankfully, I'm learning to remove the obstacles that distort my view of the world.

Thought for the Day
Sometimes we become short-sighted in our view of reality. Listening to the voice of others, and to the voice of God, can help us gain valuable new perspectives.

A Scripture for the Day
"The eye [your way of looking at things] is the lamp of the body. If your eyes are good, your whole body will be full of light. But if your eyes are bad, your whole body will be full of darkness."
- Matthew 6:22

A Prayer for the Day
"All-knowing God, unlike us, you see all aspects of life. When I get caught up in my own tunnel vision, help me to see truth as you see it, so that I might understand properly and make good choices. Amen."

DAY FORTY-TWO

Today's Sky...

Today is a typical spring day: light clouds moving across a beautiful blue sky, accented by a bright sun.

This morning I went out to enjoy a cup of coffee with a good friend at our favorite coffee shop. We had a good time. The time went fast because our conversation was positive and uplifting. I returned home, and as usual, I sat down at my kitchen table, looking out (Guess what!) my kitchen window. Right away I noticed how fast the clouds were moving. The scene changed rapidly from bright to shady. It was mesmerizing.

Thought for the Day

Change sometimes comes quickly. As the moving clouds are mesmerizing to watch, so change gives us opportunity to contemplate the events of our lives. Nature is a good teacher. So is the Word of God.

A Scripture for the Day

"Oh, how I love your law! I meditate on it all day long... I have more insight than all my teachers, for I meditate on your statutes."

- Psalm 119:97, 99

A Prayer for the Day

"Eternal Teacher, sometimes the pace of life prevents us from contemplating its meaning. Help me today to slow down and think about the truth that is revealed in nature and in your Word. Amen."

DAY FORTY-THREE

Today's Sky...

The sky is bright, producing light shade in my yard. The clouds look stationary, but they're not.

The view of my yard that I see out my kitchen window is so different from the sky. The sky looks still, but the ground view looks like a beautiful dance going on. The trees and shrubs, blown by the wind, are expressing themselves in a beautiful symphony of dance. Nature is a great choreographer.

Thought for the Day

Life is like nature. Some parts of our lives may seem slow and still, while other parts are dancing to the symphony of life. Learn from nature: don't forget to dance!

A Scripture for the Day

"You have turned my wailing into dancing; you have removed my sackcloth and clothed me with joy, that my heart may sing to you and not be silent."
- Psalm 30:11, 12

A Prayer for the Day

"Faithful God, despite the struggles of life, we have much to celebrate. Help me to live in your joy today. Amen."

DAY FORTY-FOUR

Today's Sky...

The sky is light gray and blue. It's windy again, which makes everything dance.

When I look out the big window in my patio door, I can't get enough of the view. The wooden fence that surrounds my yard limits my view but also protects the plants and shrubs and ornamental grasses, as well as my home itself, from intruders and animals.

Thought for the Day

Like my yard, I need protection on a daily basis. Good thoughts, positive thinking, and focus on God keep me from getting off track.

A Scripture for the Day

"Finally, brothers and sisters, whatever is true, whatever is noble, whatever is right, whatever is pure, whatever is lovely, whatever is admirable - if anything is excellent or praiseworthy – think about such things."
- Philippians 4:8

A Prayer for the Day

"Father God, sometimes my thoughts run away with me. Help me today to set my mind on your goodness and focus on attitudes that serve your purpose in my life. Amen."

DAY FORTY-FIVE

Today's Sky...

The sky and all the plants I see out my window look like they were born for each other.

One thing I enjoy about nature is its ability to create different scenes. The movement of the sun and clouds, along with the wind that blows the plants, cause the scene to continually change and never be the same again – ever. It's like a kaleidoscope of beauty.

Thought for the Day

You are like the sun and clouds and wind. Allow God to work with your life, and you will discover a beauty you can't even imagine.

A Scripture for the Day

"The Spirit of the Lord is upon me, because the Lord has anointed me to… comfort all who mourn, to bestow on them a crown of beauty instead of ashes, the oil of gladness instead of mourning, and a garment of praise instead of a spirit of despair."

- Isaiah 61:1, 3

A Prayer for the Day

"Loving God, sometimes I don't feel very 'beautiful.' In fact, some days I don't even like who I am. Help me today to recognize the beauty that you want to bring to my life and to be open to the work you desire to do in me. Amen."

DAY FORTY-SIX

Today's Sky...

The sky looks as if it's going to do some business today. The clouds and the thunder are saying, "Look and listen! Something great is going to happen."

Looking through my kitchen window, I'm seeing a deluge. It's wonderful to see what nature can do – providing the right conditions to water the ground. It reminds me of a mathematical equation. Everything has to be just right. Too much or too little of a single condition can affect the rain - heat, clouds, moisture, all kinds of factors. Nature has been doing this for centuries.

Thought for the Day

To accomplish any goal in life, you must pursue the right combination of factors. The proper training and education, for example, are essential in preparing for a career. In the same way, following Christ requires knowledge of His Word.

A Scripture for the Day

"Let the word of Christ dwell in you richly as you teach and admonish one another with all wisdom, and as you sing psalms, hymns and spiritual songs with gratitude in your hearts to God."
- Colossians 3:16

A Prayer for the Day

"Father God, just as we value adequate training for the development of a career, help me to allow your Word to become a part of who I am, so that I might apply its wisdom in the situations I face today. Amen."

DAY FORTY-SEVEN

Today's Sky...

The sky looks bright and shadowy due to the fast movement of the clouds.

Looking out again through my kitchen window, everything seems so orderly, which is wonderful to see. Everything I see has required time, work and sweat. This orderly appearance didn't just happen. It is like an artist painting a picture. He or she must have pallets, a canvas, and brushes to create a beautiful picture. These tools, in the hand of an artist and through the hard work of that artist produce a beautiful picture.

Thought for the Day

As the orderly view out my window is the result of time and hard work, so everything worthwhile requires commitment – time, effort, even sweat. No matter what.

A Scripture for the Day

"Forgetting what is behind and straining toward what is ahead, I press on toward the goal to win the prize for which God has called me heavenward in Christ Jesus."

- Philippians 3:13b-14

A Prayer for the Day

"Lord God, you are worthy of my deepest commitment. Help me to live for you today, even when it is difficult or inconvenient. Amen."

DAY FORTY-EIGHT

Today's Sky...

The late afternoon sky looks like it doesn't know what it wants to do. To me, it looks like the calm before the storm.

Looking out my kitchen window today, to my surprise, I notice that the grass needs cutting, even though I just mowed two days ago. I guess we've just had the right amount of rain to maximize growth. Too little rain is as bad as too much. The moisture carries the nutrition from the ground into the root systems of the grass, producing life and growth.

Thought for the Day

Life and growth require the medium of water to deliver the proper nutrients to the plant. Our bodies also require the proper amount of water. Jesus Christ is the medium through which God delivers His life-giving spiritual nutrition to our souls.

A Scripture for the Day

"Jesus said, 'If anyone is thirsty, let him come to me and drink. Whoever believes in me, as the Scripture has said, streams of living water will flow from within him.'"

- John 7:37-38

A Prayer for the Day

"Almighty God, sometimes my spirit becomes dry and thirsty. You are the source my spiritual nutrition. Let your 'living water' flow through me today, refreshing my soul. Amen."

"My green thumb came only as a result of the mistakes I made while learning to see things from the plant's point of view."

(H. Fred Ale)

DAY FORTY-NINE

Today's Sky...

The sky looks gorgeous today. What can I say? We just can't beat nature as a scene-creator.

One thing I like about nature is the different scenes it creates during the long day. The sun and clouds highlight everything I see at any given moment. (Oops, all this is happening as I sit at my kitchen window.) Nature expresses herself differently with the help of her "friends," – the sun, the clouds, even the wind.

Thought for the Day

Like nature, I too can look at my problems, and even though they're the same as yesterday, with the help of my friends, I can gain a new perspective and improve my situation. Thank God for concerned friends!

A Scripture for the Day

"Wounds from a friend can be trusted, but an enemy multiplies kisses... As iron sharpens iron, so one person sharpens another."

- Proverbs 27:6 and 27:17

A Prayer for the Day

"Thank you, Lord, for the trusted friends you have brought into my life. This day, give me the humility to receive their advice, and the sensitivity to encourage them in their struggles. Amen."

DAY FIFTY

Today's Sky…

The sky is a beautiful light blue. It's soft on the eye.

Instead of just looking out of my kitchen window, I decided today to check things out after a long day of rain. I notice that some of my plants and shrubs have holes in the leaves. Instantaneously, I yell out, "Bugs! Leaf-eater!" My plants and shrubs have an enemy – hungry bugs. Thankfully, they have me, the gardener, to rescue them. They keep their eyes on me as I walk to the shed to get (guess what) the bug pesticide. Even nature needs help to overcome her enemies!

Thought for the Day

Just as nature has enemies that threaten her well-being, so as humans we face trials and temptations that seek to bring us harm. Doctors, for example, help us with our physical issues. God himself stands ready to help us with our temptations.

A Scripture for the Day

"God is faithful; he will not let you be tempted beyond what you can bear. But when you are tempted, he will also provide a way out so that you can stand up under it."
- 1 Corinthians 10:13

A Prayer for the Day

"Holy God, you yourself are not tempted by evil and are therefore able to help us when we are tempted. I pray that when temptation comes my way, you would enable me to look to you for deliverance and faith. Amen."

DAY FIFTY-ONE

Today's Sky...

Today's sky features light clouds, and the temperature and humidity are perfect. This makes my labor easy!

The right spring temperature makes working outside comfortable. Today is near-perfect: 65-70 degrees with low humidity, which allows my body to use less energy to keep cool. This allows me to spend more time outside. In addition, the day is sunny with a light wind. What a day!

Thought for the Day

Sometimes life seems to hand us just the right conditions. Other times, we face unpleasantness and resistance. As we depend upon God's strength, we can face any conditions.

A Scripture for the Day

"Who shall separate us from the love of God? Shall trouble or hardship or persecution or famine or nakedness or danger or sword? No, in all these things we are more than conquerors through him who loved us."

- Romans 8:35, 37

A Prayer for the Day

"Faithful God, we give you thanks for the opportunities we have to enjoy pleasant conditions. Help me to trust you when life becomes difficult, and give me strength today to serve you faithfully. Amen."

DAY FIFTY-TWO

Today's Sky...

Today's sky is a beautiful blue, with white, pristine clouds and a light breeze.

As I looked out my kitchen window today, I noticed that if I wanted to keep my perfect view, I needed to cut the grass! Unlike a snapshot, this view doesn't stay the same; it requires work to keep it looking good. I find myself in a labor of love: cutting grass, removing weeds, watering plants, trimming dead flowers. But I have no regrets; it's worth it!

Thought for the Day

Following your dreams is like taking care of your yard. You may have a vision of what you want your life to be, but it requires hard work and perseverance. But don't give up; it's worth it!

A Scripture for the Day

"Where there is no vision, the people are undisciplined. But happy is the one who keeps the law (of God)."
- Proverbs 29:18

A Prayer for the Day

"Eternal God, you understand the future as well as the past. Give me a vision of what you want me to be, and help me today to make decisions that will further your purpose in my life. Amen."

DAY FIFTY-THREE

Today's Sky...

The sky looks like it wants to keep raining for a while.

When I woke up this morning, I looked out my bedroom window and noticed that the rain has saturated everything. The weight of the rain drops has caused the branches to bow. It looks as if they're bowing in surrender. However, I also know that eventually the sun will come out again, dry off the branches, and allow them to return to their normal positions. Hope seems to be built into nature itself.

Thought for the Day

Like the branches on the trees, sometimes we get bowed down with the weight of our concerns. Like the sun, God has promised us that He will sustain and restore us, so don't lose hope! The "rain" is only temporary.

A Scripture for the Day

"Do not worry, saying 'What shall we eat?' or 'What shall we drink?' or 'What shall we wear?' For...your heavenly Father knows that you need these things. But seek first his kingdom and his righteousness, and all these things (that you need) will be given to you as well."
- Matthew 6:31-33

A Prayer for the Day

"Loving God, sometimes I get discouraged, and even fearful. Help me remember today that you are the God of hope, and I can trust you for what I need. Thank you, Lord. Amen."

DAY FIFTY-FOUR

Today's Sky...

The sky looks more like a summer day than a spring one.

As I have been looking out my kitchen window over time, I have noticed that nature seems to have many surprises. However, as I observe carefully, I see that most of those "surprises" are really predictable. The plants, trees, shrubs, etc. will become what they are set to be. Their future is all contained in the seed from which they come. All will develop predictably "according to their kind."

Thought for the Day

Unlike the plants, as humans we are capable of so much more change than we often realize. We can think, rationalize, and enjoy with our five senses the depth of reality around us. Our human intelligence allows us to explore and investigate, learning and changing all the time. Life is a great adventure, isn't it?

A Scripture for the Day

"When I consider your heavens, …what is man that you are mindful of him? Yet you have made (humans) a little lower than the angels, and crowned them with glory and honor."

- Psalm 8:4-5

A Prayer for the Day

"Father God, you have created us so that we can become much more than we already are. Help me today to realize the potential you have put within me, and give me courage to change. Amen."

DAY FIFTY-FIVE

Today's Sky...

Today's sky seems to give everything a black-and-white look.

I am amazed how the sun and clouds can create a scene far more beautiful than anything we make artificially. Natural scenes are always better, and always will be. The natural, illuminated by the sun and clouds, is real. Getting in touch with nature helps us stay balanced and whole as persons.

Thought for the Day

Nature seems to be an avenue to God. It teaches us about God's wisdom and power, and by doing this, it enriches our souls. Maybe you should take a walk today, and reflect on God's creative power!

A Scripture for the Day

"The day is yours, and yours also the night; you established the sun and moon. It was you who set all the boundaries of the earth; you made both summer and winter."

- Psalm 74:16, 17

A Prayer for the Day

"Lord of Creation, the world you have made is so complex and so beautiful. Yet I often choose to live exclusively in artificial environments. Help me today to make time to experience nature itself, so that I might be reminded of your greatness. Amen."

DAY FIFTY-SIX

Today's Sky...

Today is overcast with a light rain. It's warm but not too humid.

My yard today is giving me a break. Everything seems to look beautiful and in proper order as I look out my kitchen window. I went out to have coffee with my friends, and when I came back, I decided to walk around my yard, which I really enjoy. It still looks good. It gives me comfort and a feeling of satisfaction because, after all, I am the gardener!

Thought for the Day

It's OK to stop sometimes and take pleasure in what we have accomplished. Having been created in the image of God, we find great satisfaction is creating and accomplishing things. Don't forget to celebrate your accomplishments!

A Scripture for the Day

"In the beginning God created the heavens and the earth... God saw all that he had made, and it was very good... By the seventh day God had finished the work he had been doing; so on the seventh day he rested from all his work."
- Genesis 1:1, 31; 2:2

A Prayer for the Day

"Thank you, Lord, that you have given us the capacity to be creative. Even you, Lord God, took time to stop and celebrate your accomplishments. Help me to do the same. Amen."

DAY FIFTY-SEVEN

Today's Sky...

The appearance of the sky is helping me plan my day. I appreciate that.

Nature speaks to us every day, especially through the weather. I am able to enjoy the view through my kitchen window even when the weather outside is uncomfortable. Modern science allows us to develop artificial states, especially when it comes to temperature control. All I have to do is walk down the hall and adjust the thermostat!

Thought for the Day

It has been said that there are two kinds of people in the world: "thermometers," who indicate (and complain about?) the conditions around them; and "thermostats," who influence the conditions around them. Which are you?

A Scripture for the Day

"In your hearts, set apart Christ as Lord. Always be prepared to give an answer to everyone who asks you to give the reason for the hope that you have. But do this with gentleness and respect..."

- 1 Peter 3:15

A Prayer for the Day

"Father God, forgive me for the times I have been passive about the conditions in our world. I want to make a difference for your Kingdom. Help me today to be a positive influence on the people and conditions around me. Amen."

"A great garden may have a few annoying weeds or thorns to tend to, but then, so does life."

(Byron R. Pulsifer)

DAY FIFTY-EIGHT

Today's Sky...

The sky seems to be holding in the heat and humidity.

It's another day I'm glad to have air conditioning to cool my house. The weather report for today is hot and humid all day long. And it's still springtime! There is one part of my yard which needs more care than the rest. It's my grass, and today it needs to be cut. I must do it today because tomorrow's forecast is possible showers. Wet grass is hard to cut. Despite the humidity, I've discovered that if I stop often to drink water, the heat and humidity is bearable. So refreshing!

Thought for the Day

Just as our bodies are designed to need physical water, so our souls need the refreshment of spiritual "water." Jesus taught us that He could provide life-giving refreshment. All we have to do is receive it!

A Scripture for the Day

"Jesus answered, 'Everyone who drinks this (well) water will be thirsty again, but whoever drinks the water I give him will never thirst. Indeed, the water I give him will become in him a spring of water welling up to eternal life."

- John 4:13-14

A Prayer for the Day

"Lord Jesus, you are the source of spiritual refreshment and vitality. Help me today to drink of the abundant supply that you have offered us. Renew my soul. Amen."

DAY FIFTY-NINE

Today's Sky...

The sky has a calm, shadowy look today, with a very light rain. Nature can be calm.

Now and then I like to relax no matter what is happening. A day of reflection is nice and renewing. Looking out my kitchen window, I love the calmness I see outside. Even though it's raining slightly, there is practically no wind. It's not a bright day, but it still has a beauty of its own.

Thought for the Day

As calmness has a place in nature, so I need to seek calmness in my life more often. The essence of faith is being calm and allowing God to control the outcomes in your life.

A Scripture for the Day

"Therefore I tell you, do not worry about your life, what you will eat or drink; or about your body, what you will wear. Is not life more important than food, and the body more important than clothes?"

- Matthew 6:25

A Prayer for the Day

"Lord God, I often get so busy that I forget to trust you. Sometimes I worry needlessly about the events of my life. Teach me to let go of my striving and allow you to be in charge. Amen."

DAY SIXTY

Today's Sky...
It's another gray-looking day, but the gray has a beauty of its own.

I never thought about how wonderful colors are in expressing life, especially in the natural realm. There are so many varieties of colors; even different shades of similar colors. The combination of these colors gives my garden its distinctive beauty. The different colors of the sky and the plants can affect our state of mind. All colors are beautiful in their own right.

Thought for the Day
Just as nature's pallet gives the scenes around us the depth and texture that create beauty, our moods and emotions bring beauty to our lives. Affirming some of these moods and denying others limits the fulfillment that we experience. We celebrate life more fully when we welcome all different kinds of feelings.

A Scripture for the Day
"O Lord, you have examined me and you know me... Search me, O God, and know my heart; test me and know my anxious thoughts. See if there is any offensive way in me, and lead me in the way everlasting."

- Psalm 139:1, 23-24

A Prayer for the Day
"Father God, thank you for this journey I have been on these past two months. I pray that you would enable me to be honest with you in the days ahead, so that you can transform every aspect of my being, and bring me into your love and peace. Amen."

Made in the USA
Columbia, SC
31 October 2021